HELLO KITTY®
288 Page Coloring
& Activity Book

W9-AHF-444

Bendon Publishing International, Inc.
Ashland, OH 44805
www.bendonpub.com

Home Sweet Home!

Which Picture is Different?

1.

2.

3.

4.

Answers in the back.

Finish the Picture
Finish drawing the sunflower.

Who Is Hiding?

Hello Kitty is waiting at the cafe for one of her friends.
Color in the spaces using the special color code
at the bottom of the page to find out who it is!

★ = pink   ✴ = light pink   ◉ = yellow

● = red   ♥ = blue   ■ = brown   ▲ = black

Supermarket

After school, Hello Kitty rides her bicycle to the supermarket.

HOW MANY?

Count the items below and
place your answer on the line.

_____ ORANGES.

Which Picture is Different?

1.

2.

3.

4.

Answers in the back.

I love you!

HELLO KITTY®

Garden

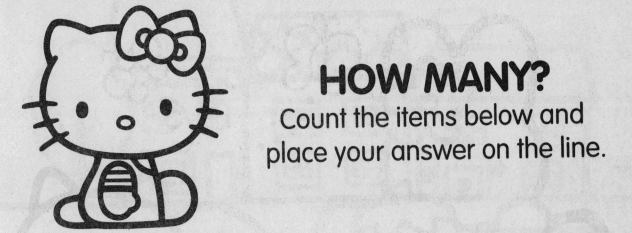

HOW MANY?

Count the items below and place your answer on the line.

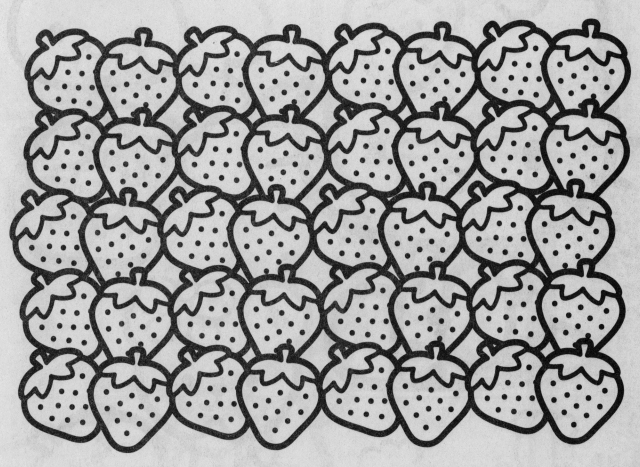

_____ STRAWBERRIES.

Hello Kitty sends a letter to Tracy.

Connect the dots to see who has a special delivery!

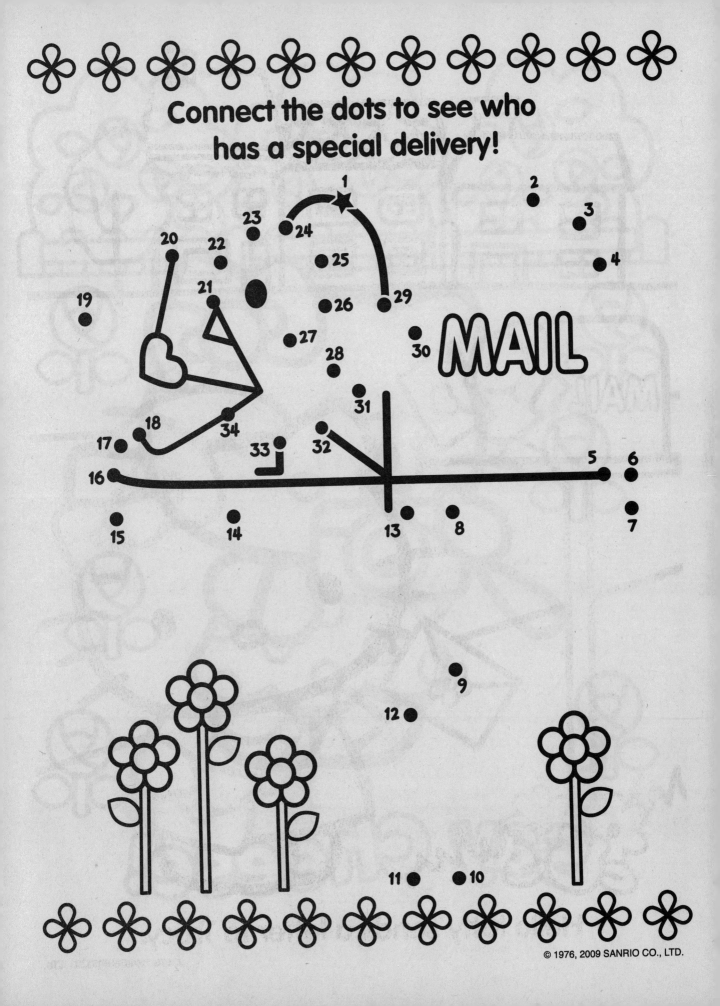

Say Cheese!

Mama

My Family

Papa

Mimmy

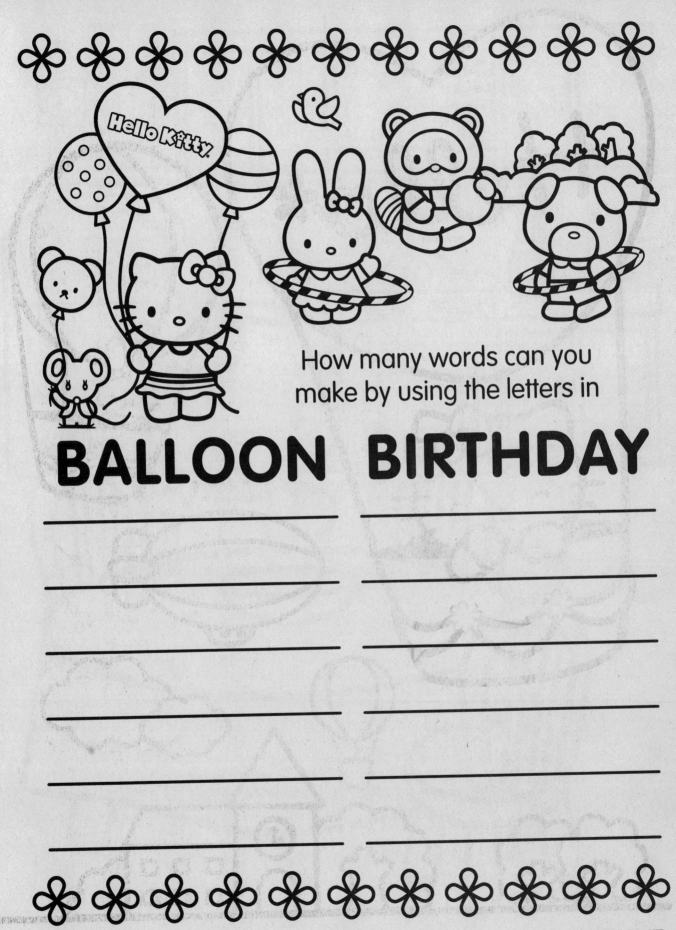

How many words can you make by using the letters in

BALLOON BIRTHDAY

HELLO KITTY'S PEPPERMINT PIE

ADULT ASSISTANCE IS STRONGLY ADVISED.

INGREDIENTS

- 24 chocolate wafer cookies, crushed
- 1/2 cup butter
- 3 cups miniature marshmallows
- 1/2 cup milk
- 1 cup heavy whipping cream
- 1/2 cup crushed peppermint hard candies
- RED FOOD COLORING

DIRECTIONS

1. Combine cookies and melted butter or margarine. Press into 9 inch pie plate. Bake at 350 degrees F (175 degrees C) for 10 minutes. Cool.

2. Put 3 cups marshmallows in a double boiler. Add milk, and cook until mixture melts and thickens. Cool in refrigerator for about 15 minutes.

3. In another bowl, whip the cream. Blend in the crushed candy and add one drop red food coloring. Fold whipped cream mixture into melted and cooled marshmallow mixture.

4. Pour into crust, and chill well before serving.

My Friends

Jody   Tippy

Lorry

Joey

Tracy   Thomas

Tim and Tammy

The flower shop always has lovely things!

HOW MANY?

Count the items below and
place your answer on the line.

_____ COOKIES.

© 1976, 2009 SANRIO CO., LTD.

Finish the Picture
Finish drawing Mama.

Hello Kitty is looking for her other shoe.
Find and circle the shoe that matches.

Answers in the back.

WHICH IS WHICH?

Draw a line from each shadow to the
character to which it belongs.

Answers in the back.

HELLO KITTY®
SQUARES

Taking turns, connect a line from one heart to another. Whoever makes the line that completes a box puts their initials inside the box. The person with the most squares at the end of the game wins!

EXAMPLE:

Hello Kitty loves the outdoors!

Hello Kitty likes to visit Farmer Brown's farm.

Hello Kitty does her chores.

Connect the dots to see what Hello Kitty is doing on the farm!

Farmer Brown's Farm

Can you help Hello Kitty follow the apples to find her way to Farmer Brown's house?

←FINISH

START

© 1976, 2009 SANRIO CO., LTD.

Color by Letter

Using the key below as a guide, finish
the picture of Hello Kitty and Lorry.

A=Green B=Blue C=Yellow D=White
E=Orange F=Red G=Brown

Hello Kitty's friends like visiting
the library to check out books.

**Reading is fun, but remember
to be quiet in the library!**

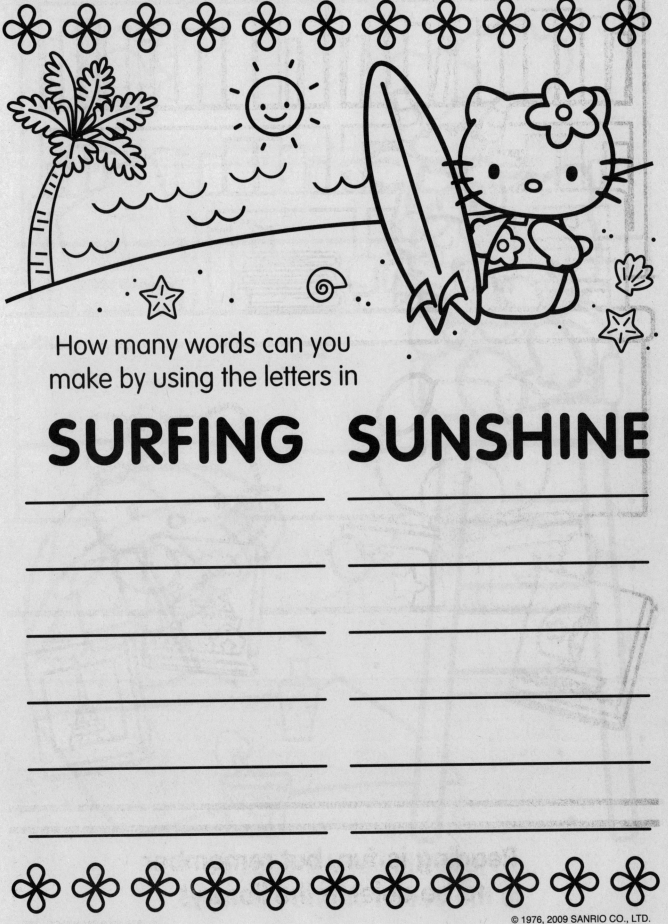

How many words can you make by using the letters in

SURFING SUNSHINE

_____   _____

_____   _____

_____   _____

_____   _____

_____   _____

_____   _____

Hello Kitty and friends go
to the beach on the weekend.

A warm day at the beach.

Let's hula on the sand!

Fifi and kathy wear sunscreen lotion.

Look at all the pretty flowers Hello Kitty planted!

HELLO KITTY® SQUARES

Taking turns, connect a line from one flower to another. Whoever makes the line that completes a box puts their initials inside the box. The person with the most squares at the end of the game wins!

Mr. Policeman directs traffic in Hello Kitty's neighborhood.

There is a fire station in Hello Kitty's neighborhood.

Fight the Fire!

Help Hello Kitty and her fire fighting friends put out the fire. Find the way from the fire hydrant to the flames.

Answers in the back.

Making pretty music is fun!

WHICH IS WHICH?

Draw a line from each shadow to the character to which it belongs.

Answers in the back.

Finish the Picture
Finish drawing Dear Daniel.

TREASURE HUNT

Hello kitty needs to find all of the items on the list below
to put into the box. Can you find and circle all 8 items?

FIND SOMETHING SPARKLY. FIND SOMETHING WITH PETALS.

FIND SOMETHING THAT FLIES. FIND SOMETHING THAT FLOATS.

FIND A CIRCLE. FIND A STAR.

FIND A HEXAGON. FIND SOMETHING TO WEAR.

Answers in Back

So Sweet!

HOW MANY?

Count the items below and place your answer on the line.

_____ NOTES.

Hello Kitty School Code

Hello Kitty wrote a note for you in secret code. Can you read the message? Use the Code Key below.

Code Key:

🌸 = S   📖 = u   🍎 = N   ✕ = d

✂ = a   ✏ = i   🖌 = g   □ = e

⭐ = r   👓 = f

Secret Message:

Let's Cook!

I love you!

HELLO KITTY®

HELLO KITTY®

Hello Kitty®

Tic-Tac-Toe
Fun!

Finish the Picture

Kathy loves to go to the beach.
Connect the dots and then color the picture.

Answers in the back.

Hello Kitty®

So Sweet!

Grandpa

Grandma

Which Picture is Different?

1.

2.

3.

4.

Answers in the back.

What does Hello Kitty need for this sport?

Connect the dots to see!

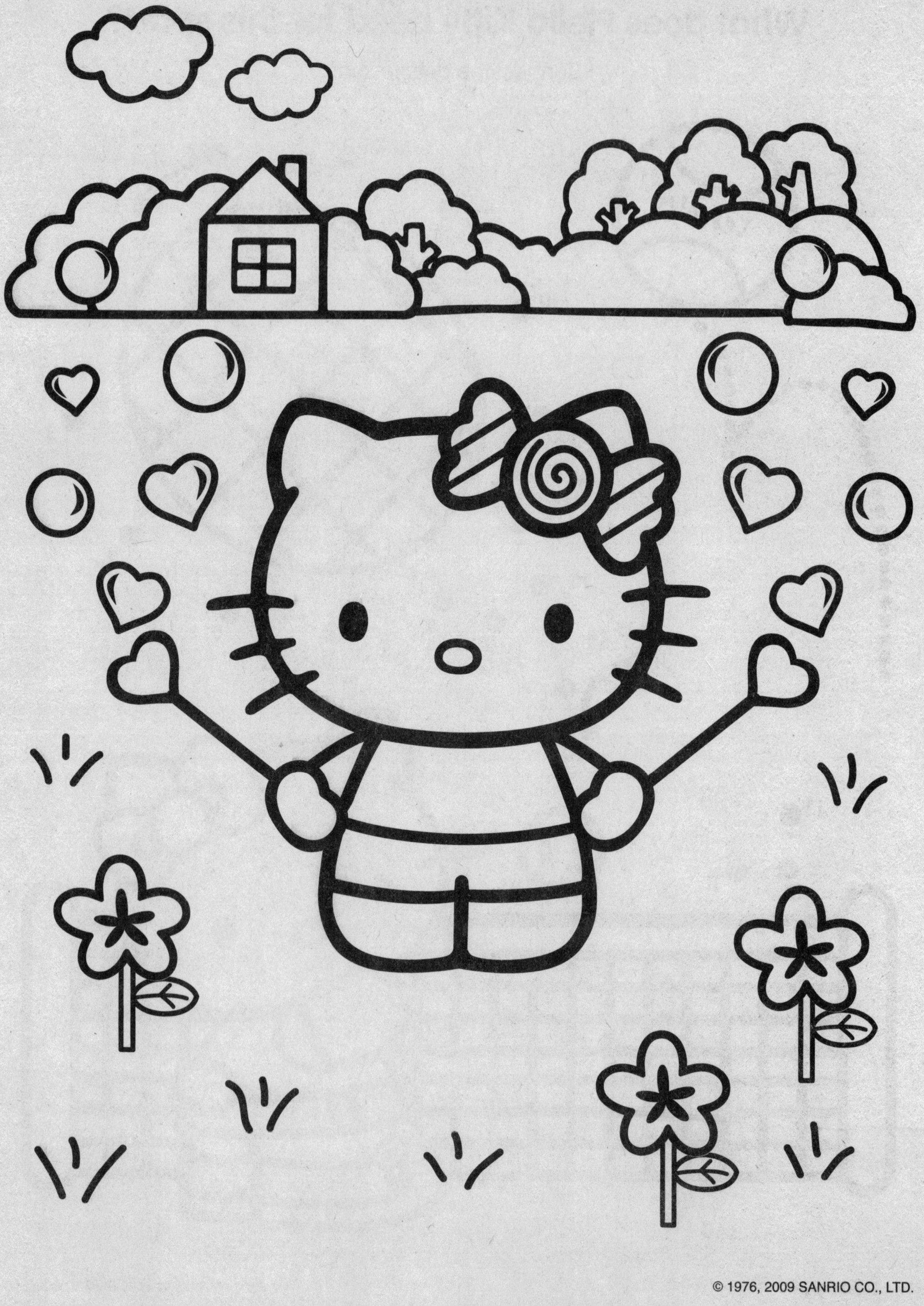

Pogo Race!

Can you figure out which path Hello Kitty, Tracy, and Kathy bounced on with each of their pogo sticks?

Start 1

Start 2

Start 3

Flower Find!

Can you find the 11 flowers that are hidden in the picture? Circle the flowers as you find them.

Answers in the back.

Let's Dance!

Buzzy Bee!

Hello Kitty®

Tic-Tac-Toe Fun!

Which Picture is Different?

Answers in the back.

© 1976, 2009 SANRIO CO., LTD.

Help the bus driver find his way to the school!

SCHOOL BUS

SCHOOL

Answer in the back.

© 1976, 2009 SANRIO CO., LTD.

Find the Match
Draw a line from each character
to his or her name.

Thomas

Hello Kitty®

Mimmy

Jody

Answers in the back.

Hello Kitty is always sure to brush her teeth.

A cup of tea and a biscuit are always nice.

Help the waiter find his way to Hello Kitty's table.

Answer in the back.

TREASURE HUNT

Hello Kitty needs to find all of the items on the list below to put into the box. Can you find and circle all 8 items?

FIND SOMETHING ROUND. FIND SOMETHING SWEET.

FIND SOMETHING TO WEAR. FIND SOMETHING THAT HOPS .

FIND A FLOWER. FIND AN APPLE .

FIND A HEART . FIND SOMETHING THAT RINGS.

Answers in the back.

Find the Pair

Hello Kitty would like to buy some shoes...but they are all mixed up! Help her find the ONE pair of matching shoes by drawing a line from one shoe to the other. Look carefully! The shoes have to be an EXACT match.

Answers in the back.

Finish the Picture
Finish drawing Kathy.

Hello Kitty loves to go skating!

Find the Match

Draw a line from each character to his or her name.

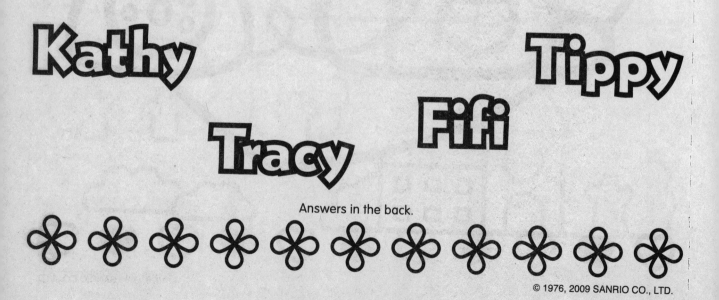

Kathy

Tracy

Fifi

Tippy

Answers in the back.

BAKERY

Can you figure out which route Hello Kitty flew in her airplane?

Route 1

Route 2

Route 3

Route 4

Answers in the back.

Mimmy

My
Family

Mama

Papa

Hello Kitty and her friends like to play croquet in the park.

Everyone takes a turn.

**Hello Kitty and her friends spend
a fun-filled day at the amusement park.**

They also like to have picnics

and ride bikes in the park too.

Hello Kitty®

Tic-Tac-Toe Fun!

HELLO KITTY®

Have a parent or caregiver cut out the puzzle pieces on the dotted lines. Mix up the pieces, and put the picture back together!

PUZZLE

ENGLISH DAISY

Welcome to Hello Kitty's Neighborhood!

Hello Kitty's house has a red roof.

This is
Hello Kitty's bedroom.

How many words can you
make by using the letters in

MUSIC NOTES

Hello Kitty®

Tic-Tac-Toe Fun!

How Many Butterflies?

Help Hello Kitty find the butterflies.
Circle and count the butterflies.

Answers in the back.

How many words can you make by using the letters in

FLOWER   BOUQUET

_____   _____

_____   _____

_____   _____

_____   _____

_____   _____

_____   _____

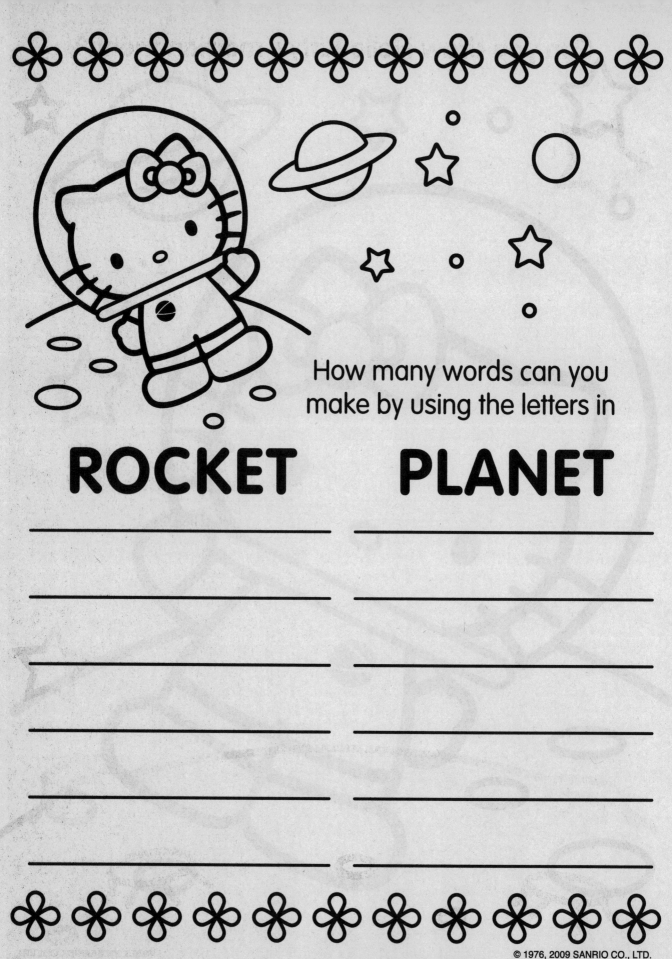

How many words can you make by using the letters in

ROCKET   PLANET

_____   _____

_____   _____

_____   _____

_____   _____

_____   _____

_____   _____

Can you draw Hello Kitty's martian friend?

HOW MANY?

Count the items below and place your answer on the line.

_____ STARS.

Hello Kitty and Fifi share some time together.

HELLO KITTY® SQUARES

Taking turns, connect a line from one star to another. Whoever makes the line that completes a box puts their initials inside the box. The person with the most squares at the end of the game wins!

EXAMPLE:

☆—☆ ☆
A
☆—☆ ☆

☆—☆ ☆

☆ ☆ ☆ ☆ ☆ ☆ ☆ ☆ ☆ ☆ ☆ ☆ ☆ ☆
☆ ☆ ☆ ☆ ☆ ☆ ☆ ☆ ☆ ☆ ☆ ☆ ☆ ☆
☆ ☆ ☆ ☆ ☆ ☆ ☆ ☆ ☆ ☆ ☆ ☆ ☆ ☆
☆ ☆ ☆ ☆ ☆ ☆ ☆ ☆ ☆ ☆ ☆ ☆ ☆ ☆
☆ ☆ ☆ ☆ ☆ ☆ ☆ ☆ ☆ ☆ ☆ ☆ ☆ ☆
☆ ☆ ☆ ☆ ☆ ☆ ☆ ☆ ☆ ☆ ☆ ☆ ☆ ☆
☆ ☆ ☆ ☆ ☆ ☆ ☆ ☆ ☆ ☆ ☆ ☆ ☆ ☆
☆ ☆ ☆ ☆ ☆ ☆ ☆ ☆ ☆ ☆ ☆ ☆ ☆ ☆
☆ ☆ ☆ ☆ ☆ ☆ ☆ ☆ ☆ ☆ ☆ ☆ ☆ ☆
☆ ☆ ☆ ☆ ☆ ☆ ☆ ☆ ☆ ☆ ☆ ☆ ☆ ☆
☆ ☆ ☆ ☆ ☆ ☆ ☆ ☆ ☆ ☆ ☆ ☆ ☆ ☆

Color by Letter

Using the key below as a guide, finish
the picture of Hello Kitty.

A=Green   B=Blue   C=Yellow   D=White
E=Orange   F=Red   G=Brown

WHICH IS WHICH?

Draw a line from each shadow to the character to which it belongs.

Answers in the back.

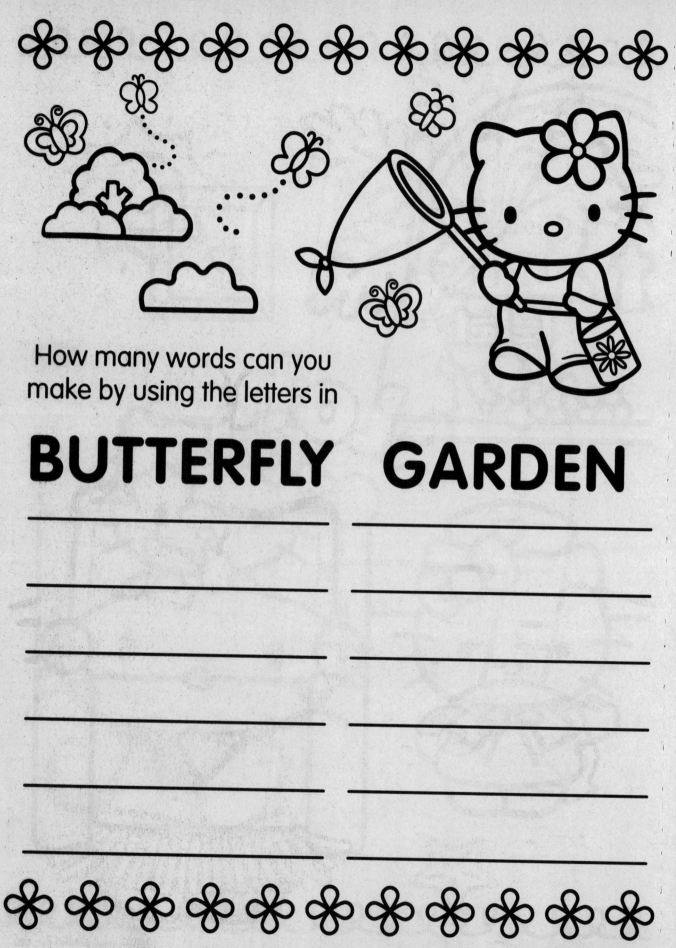

How many words can you
make by using the letters in

BUTTERFLY GARDEN

_____   _____

_____   _____

_____   _____

_____   _____

_____   _____

_____   _____

Aloha!

Finish the Picture

Connect the dots and then color the picture.

Let's go for a swim!

Surf's Up!
Can you help Hello Kitty find her way back to the beach?

End

Start

Have a parent or caregiver cut out the puzzle pieces on the dotted lines. Mix up the pieces, and put the picture back together!

PUZZLE

Hello Kitty®

Tic-Tac-Toe Fun!

HOW MANY?

Count the items below and
place your answer on the line.

_____ **BALLOONS.**

WHICH IS WHICH?

Draw a line from each shadow to the
character to which it belongs.

Answers in the back.

HOW MANY?

Count the items below and place your answer on the line.

_____ HEARTS.

Hello Kitty

HOW MANY?

Count the items below and place your answer on the line.

_____ FLOWERS.

WINTER FUN!

Can you find these words in the word search?

igloo
snowman
fort
sledding
skating
ice
snowboard

```
h e c i n c q x v s
y a c m n u w f g n
z s t i k x t o b o
s n o w b o a r d w
r c l u o y r t c m
x e o l a v w m q a
c z g n i t a k s n
t i s l e d d i n g
```

HOW MANY?

Count the items below and place your answer on the line.

_____ MITTENS.

ARRIVAL

1			
2			
3			
4			
5			

DEPARTURE

1			
2			
3			
4			
5			

Hello Kitty and her parents get ready to take a trip.

Flower Power
Can you match the flowers to the right pots?

Bath time!

© 1976, 2009 SANRIO CO., LTD.

Children's Matinee

Tickets

Hello Kitty's neighborhood has a movie theater.

Fresh Hot
Popcorn

butter

S

Draw a scene from your favorite movie on the movie screen!

Movie Time Fun!

Can you find all of the words listed below in the puzzle?
Look up, down, left, right, and diagonal!

popcorn   soda   candy
friends   laugh   movie
actress   star   ticket
sound effects   dancing   singing
matinee   chocolate bar   theater

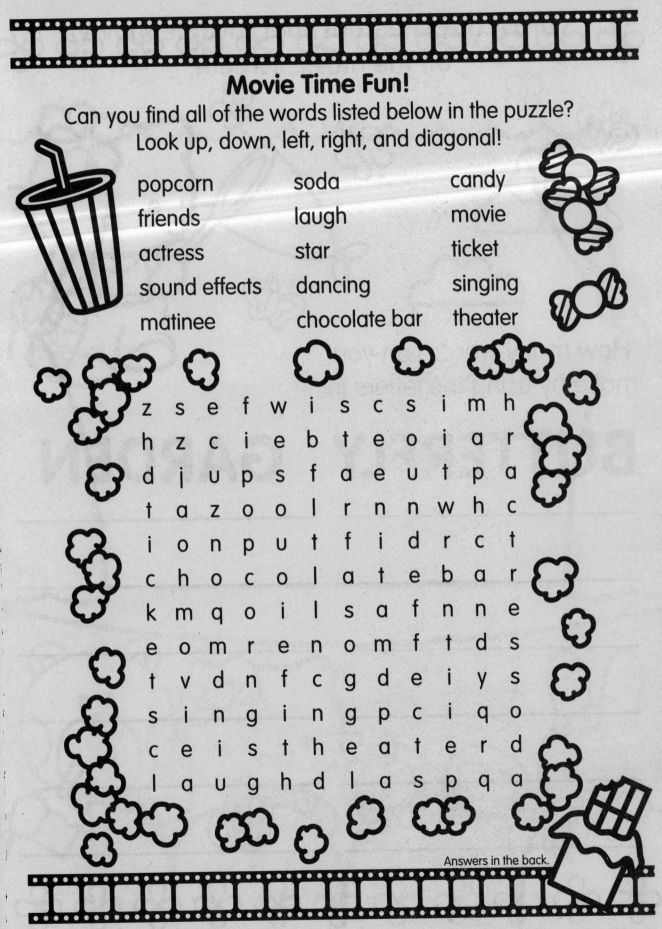

```
z s e f w i s c s i m h
h z c i e b t e o i a r
d j u p s f a e u t p a
t a z o o l r n n w h c
i o n p u t f i d r c t
c h o c o l a t e b a r
k m q o i l s a f n n e
e o m r e n o m f t d s
t v d n f c g d e i y s
s i n g i n g p c i q o
c e i s t h e a t e r d
l a u g h d l a s p q a
```

Answers in the back.

How many words can you
make by using the letters in

BUTTERFLY GARDEN

Time For Bed

It's time for bed but Hello Kitty can't find her teddy bear!
Find and circle the teddy bear.

Answers in the back.

Draw a portrait
of your best friend!

Hello Kitty Mask

ASK AN ADULT FOR HELP WITH THIS ACTIVITY!

What you will need:

Scissors
Glue stick
Popsicle stick
Paper plate
Tape

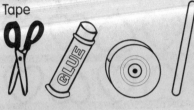

Directions:

1. Color the picture.
2. Cut along the dotted line (with adult supervision!)
3. Paste the picture to the center of the paper plate.
4. Tape popsicle stick to the back of the paper plate.
5. You're Hello Kitty!

How many words can you make by using the letters in

LIBRARY   READING

Can you find the crayon set that matches?

1

2

3

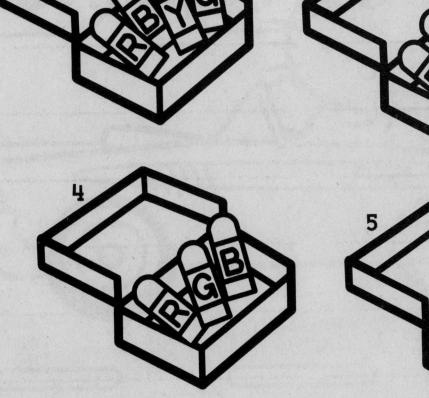

4

5

SCHO

BUS
STOP

HELLO KITTY® SQUARES

Taking turns, connect a line from one apple to another. Whoever makes the line that completes a box puts their initials inside the box. The person with the most squares at the end of the game wins!

EXAMPLE:

Unscramble the List

What did Hello Kitty buy at the store?
Unscramble the words on her grocery list to find out!

Grocery List

ikml   _ _ _ _

rnaoeg iecuj   _ _ _ _ _ _ _ _ _ _

radeb   _ _ _ _ _

paleps   _ _ _ _ _ _

rocrats   _ _ _ _ _ _ _

bristwerasre   _ _ _ _ _ _ _ _ _ _ _

rgpase   _ _ _ _ _ _

Fresh Baked

2.5 6

Fresh baked cookies from the bakery are delicious.

Hello Kitty wants to pick out a new dress.

Hello Kitty loves to shop at all her favorite stores.

HELLO KITTY'S PINK PUNCH

ADULT ASSISTANCE IS STRONGLY ADVISED.

INGREDIENTS

2 liters ginger ale
2 liters cranberry juice
1 gallon raspberry sorbet

DIRECTIONS

1. In a large punch bowl, mix 1 liter chilled ginger ale and 1 liter chilled cranberry juice. Next, scoop raspberry sorbet into the bowl. Then pour remaining chilled ginger ale and cranberry juice over sorbet.

candy

HOW MANY?

Count the items below and
place your answer on the line.

_____ BUTTERFLIES.

Fifi sits behind Hello Kitty at school.

Can you spot 10 differences between this page and the one before it?

Which Picture is Different?

1.

2.

3.

4.

Answers in the back.

© 1976, 2009 SANRIO CO., LTD.

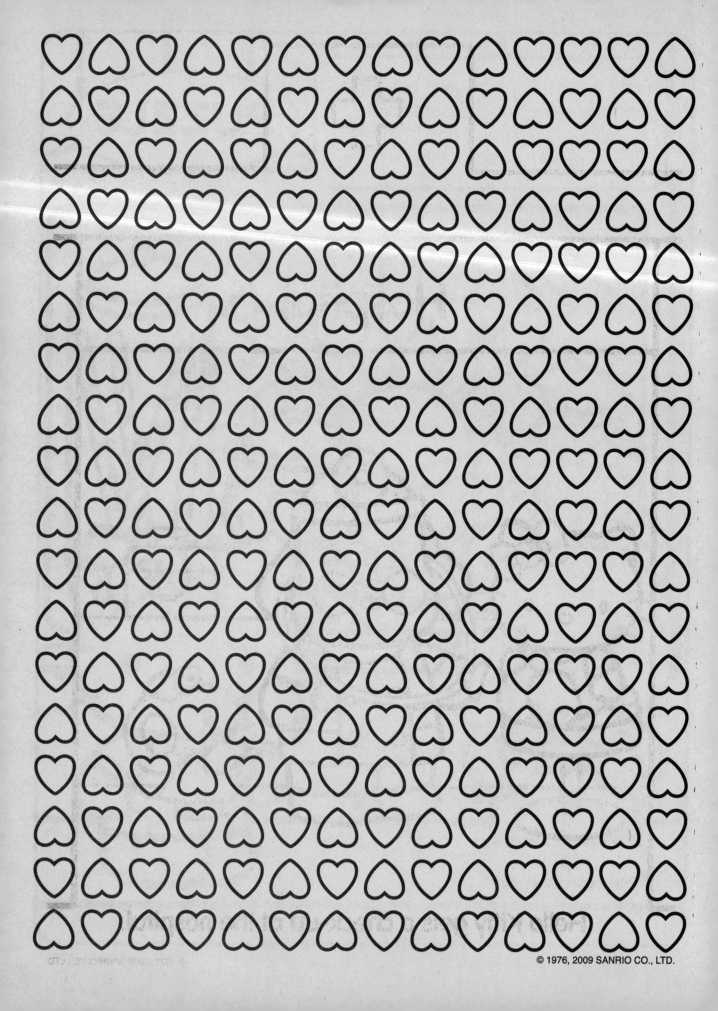

Hospital

Hello Kitty gets a check-up at the hospital.

Hello Kitty sends a letter to her pen pal.

STRAWBERRY

Flower Bouquet

Help Hello Kitty finish picking out flowers to put in the bouquet she is going to give Mama. First, connect the dots and then color in the pretty picture.

Hello Kitty and Fifi play together.

Museum Word Find

Can you find all of these museum words in the word find?
Look up, down, right, left, and diagonal!

artwork

dinosaurs

fossils

painting

sculpture

prehistoric

quiet

learn

history

school

scientist

artist

l	e	a	r	n	l	w	s	l	l	z	f
w	p	a	r	p	t	n	c	c	k	c	o
s	v	s	p	t	a	l	i	d	w	y	s
i	b	c	l	z	i	i	e	l	r	w	s
a	x	u	u	r	c	s	n	o	q	r	i
n	a	l	s	o	h	p	t	t	u	e	l
v	r	p	s	p	c	s	i	a	i	r	s
m	t	t	l	c	i	z	s	i	e	n	J
i	w	u	a	h	h	o	t	w	t	p	g
d	o	r	l	l	n	o	t	w	p	v	k
p	r	e	h	i	s	t	o	r	i	c	g
f	k	m	d	f	e	c	w	l	k	y	q

Answers in the back.

Petting animals at the zoo is always exciting!

There are so many cute animals at the zoo!

Mimmy, Fifi, Kathy and Hello Kitty

practice ballet in front of a mirror.

How many words can you make by using the letters in

DANCING TWIRLING

_____   _____

_____   _____

_____   _____

_____   _____

_____   _____

_____   _____

COTTON
CANDY

✿ Answers ✿

✿✿✿✿✿✿✿✿✿✿✿
Which Picture is Different?

✿✿✿✿✿✿✿✿✿✿✿

✿✿✿✿✿✿✿✿✿✿✿
Which Picture is Different?

✿✿✿✿✿✿✿✿✿✿✿

Good Morning!

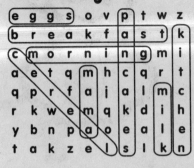

✿✿✿✿✿✿✿✿✿
Finish the Picture
Connect the dots and then color the picture.

✿✿✿✿✿✿✿✿✿

Hello Kitty is looking for her other shoe.
Find and circle the shoe that matches.

✿✿✿✿✿✿✿✿✿
WHICH IS WHICH?
Draw a line from each shadow to the
character to which it belongs.

✿✿✿✿✿✿✿✿✿

✿✿✿✿✿✿✿✿✿
Farmer Brown's Farm
Can you help Hello Kitty follow the apples to
find her way Farmer Brown's house?

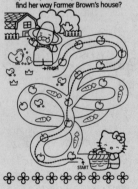

✿✿✿✿✿✿✿✿✿

Fight the Fire!
Help Hello Kitty and her fire fighting
friends put out the fire. Find the way
from the fire hydrant to the flames.

Twin Policemen!
Can you spot the twins?
Which two policemen are
exactly the same?

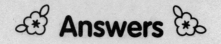

WHICH IS WHICH?
Draw a line from each shadow to the character to which it belongs.

TREASURE HUNT
Hello kitty needs to find all of the items on the list below to put into the box. Can you find and circle all 8 items?

FIND SOMETHING SPARKLY.   FIND SOMETHING WITH PETALS.
FIND SOMETHING THAT FLIES. FIND SOMETHING THAT FLOATS.
FIND A CIRCLE.   FIND A STAR.
FIND A HEXAGON.   FIND SOMETHING TO WEAR.

Hello Kitty School Code
Hello Kitty wrote a note for you in secret code. Can you read the message? Use the Code Key below.

Finish the Picture
Kathy loves to go to the beach. Connect the dots and then color the picture.

Answers in the back.

Which Picture is Different?

Answers in the back.

Flower Find!
Can you find the 11 flowers that are hidden in the picture? Circle the flowers as you find them.

Which Picture is Different?

Answers in the back.

Help the bus driver find his way to the school!

SCHOOL BUS

SCHOOL

Answer in the back.

Find the Match
Draw a line from each character to his or her name.

Thomas   Hello Kitty

Mimmy   Jody

Answers in the back.

✸ Answers ✸

Help the waiter find his way to Hello Kitty's table.

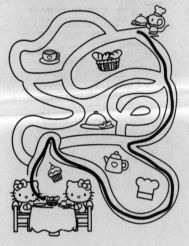

TREASURE HUNT

Hello Kitty needs to find all of the items on the list below to put into the box. Can you find and circle all 8 items?

FIND SOMETHING ROUND.   FIND SOMETHING SWEET.
FIND SOMETHING TO WEAR.   FIND SOMETHING THAT HOPS.
FIND A FLOWER.   FIND AN APPLE.
FIND A HEART.   FIND SOMETHING THAT RINGS.

Find the Pair

Hello Kitty would like to buy some shoes...but they are all mixed up! Help her find the ONE pair of matching shoes by drawing a line from one shoe to the other. Look carefully! The shoes have to be an EXACT match.

Find the Match

Draw a line from each character to his or her name.

Kathy   Tippy
Tracy   Fifi

Answers in the back.

Can you figure out which route Hello Kitty flew in her airplane?

Route 1   Route 2   Route 4   Route 3

How Many Butterflies?

Help Hello Kitty find the butterflies. Circle and count the butterflies.

Answer: 10 Butterflies

WHICH IS WHICH?

Draw a line from each shadow to the character to which it belongs.

Surf's Up!

Can you help Hello Kitty find her way back to the beach?

End

Start

WHICH IS WHICH?

Draw a line from each shadow to the character to which it belongs.

Answers in the back.

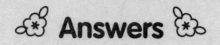

Answers

WINTER FUN!

```
h e c i n c q x v s
y a c m n u w f g n
z s t i k x t o b o
s n o w b o a r d w
r c l u o y r t c m
x e o l a v w m q a
c z g n i t a k s n
t i s l e d d i n g
```

Movie Time Fun!

```
z s e f w i s c s i m h
h z c i e b t e o i a r
d i u p s f a e u t p a
t a z o o l r n w h c t
i o n p u t f i d r c t
c h o c o l a t e b a r
k m q o i l s a f n n e
k e o m r e n o m f t d
t v d n f c g d e i y s
s i n g i n g p c i q o
c e i s t h e a t e r d
l a u g h d l a s p q a
```

❋❋❋❋❋❋❋❋

Time For Bed

It's time for bed but Hello Kitty can't find her teddy bear! Find and circle the teddy bear.

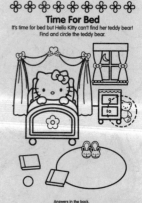

Answers in the back.

❋❋❋❋❋❋❋❋

Unscramble the List

ikml <u>milk</u>

rnaoeg iecuj <u>orange juice</u>

radeb <u>bread</u>

paleps <u>apples</u>

rocrats <u>carrots</u>

bristwerasre <u>strawberries</u>

rgpase <u>grapes</u>

Can you spot 10 differences between this page and the one before it?

Which Picture is Different?

1.   2.
3.   4.

Museum Word Find

```
l e a r n l w s l l z f
w p a r p t t c c k c o
s v s p t a l i d w y s
i b c l z i i e l r w s
a x u u c c s n o q r i
n a l s o h p t t u e l
v r p s p c s i a i r s
m t t l c i z i s i e n
i w u a h h o t w t p o
d o r l n o t w p v k
p r e h i s t o r i c g
f k m d f e c w l k y q
```

Make-Over Time!

1. <u>shampoo</u>
2. <u>beauty parlor</u>
3. <u>nail polish</u>
4. <u>conditioner</u>
5. <u>curly</u>
6. <u>perfume</u>
7. <u>scissors</u>
8. <u>brush</u>

A makeover makes Hello Kitty feel like a <u>princess</u>.